Comparing Past and Present

Going to the Doctor

Rebecca Rissman

Edited by Rebecca Rissman, Daniel Nunn, and Catherine Veitch
Designed by Philippa Jenkins
Picture research by Elizabeth Alexander
Production by Helen McCreath
Originated by Capstone Global Library Ltd
Printed and bound in China

ISBN 978 1 4062 7148 5
17 16 15 14 13
10 9 8 7 6 5 4 3 2 1

British Library Cataloguing in Publication Data
A full catalogue record for this book is available from the British Library.

Acknowledgements
We would like to thank the following for permission to reproduce photographs: Alamy pp. 5 (© YAY Media AS), 7 (© Tetra Images), 8 (© Old Visuals), 9 (© Blend Images), 11 (© jozef mikietyn), 23 (© jozef mikietyn); Corbis pp. 6 (© Alinari Archives), 16 (© H Bedford Lemere/English Heritage), 18 (© Bettmann), 23 (© H Bedford Lemere/English Heritage); Getty Images pp. 4 (A. R. Coster/Topical Press Agency/Hulton Archive), 10 (Fox Photos/Hulton Archive), 12 (Vintage Images), 17 (Halfdark/the Agency Collection), 23 (Halfdark/the Agency Collection); Mary Evans p. 14 (Sueddeutsche Zeitung Photo); Shutterstock pp. 13 (© CandyBox Images), 15 (© mangostock), 19 (© wavebreakmedia), 21 (© Monkey Business Images), 23 (© wavebreakmedia); SuperStock pp. 20 (ClassicStock.com), 22.

Front cover photographs of a sick child receiving a bunch of daffodils reproduced with permission of Getty Images (Fox Photos/Hulton Archive), and a doctor checking a child patient reproduced with permission of Getty Images (SelectStock/the Agency Collection). Back cover photograph of a doctor talking to a patient reproduced with permission of Superstock.

We would like to thank Nancy Harris and Diana Bentley for their invaluable help in the preparation of this book.

Every effort has been made to contact copyright holders of material reproduced in this book. Any omissions will be rectified in subsequent printings if notice is given to the publisher.

Contents

Comparing the past and present 4

Seeing the doctor 8

Getting to the doctor 10

Medicine 14

Hospitals 16

Doctors and nurses 18

Then and now 22

Picture glossary 23

Index 24

Notes for parents and teachers 24

Comparing the past and present

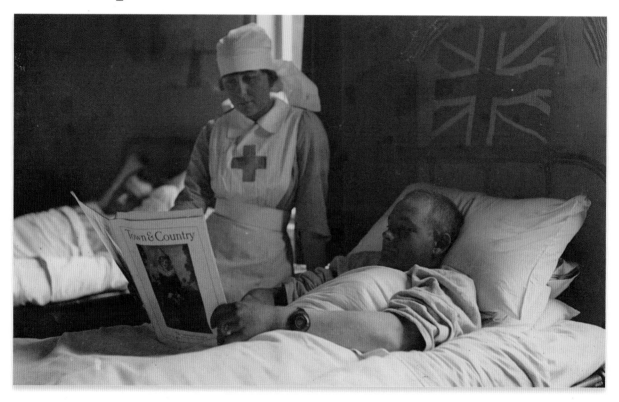

Things in the past have already happened.

Things in the present are happening now.

5

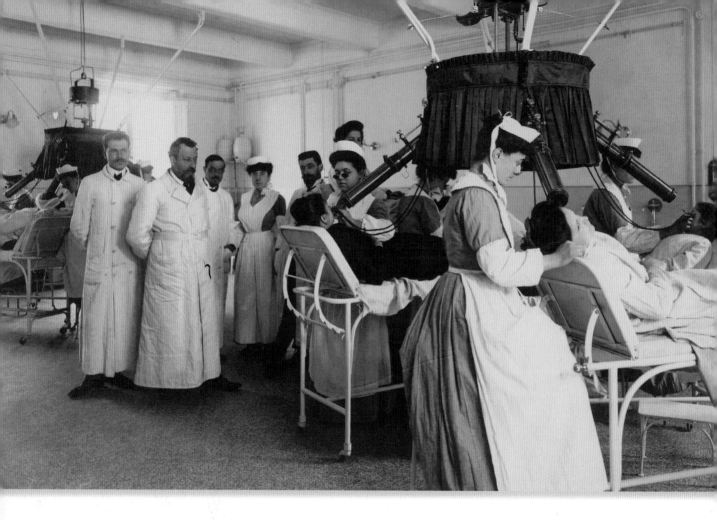

Going to the doctor has changed over time.

The way people go to the doctor today is very different to the past.

Seeing the doctor

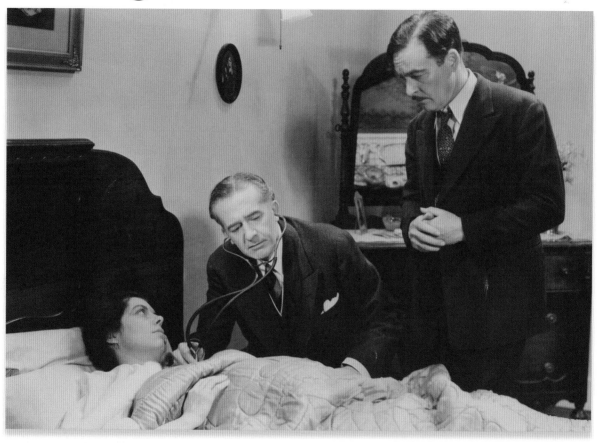

In the past some doctors visited the homes of sick people.

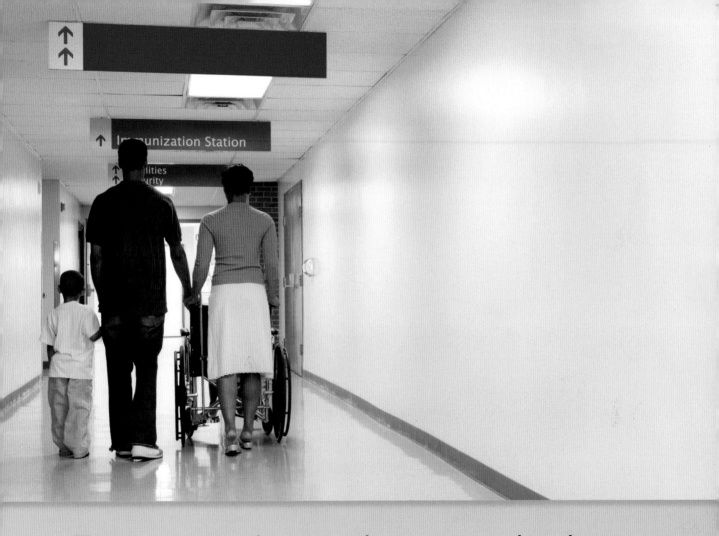

Today, most people see a doctor at a hospital or surgery.

Getting to the doctor

In the past some people went
a long way to see the doctor.

Today, most people live close to a doctor's surgery or hospital.

In the past some sick people went to the hospital in ambulance carts.

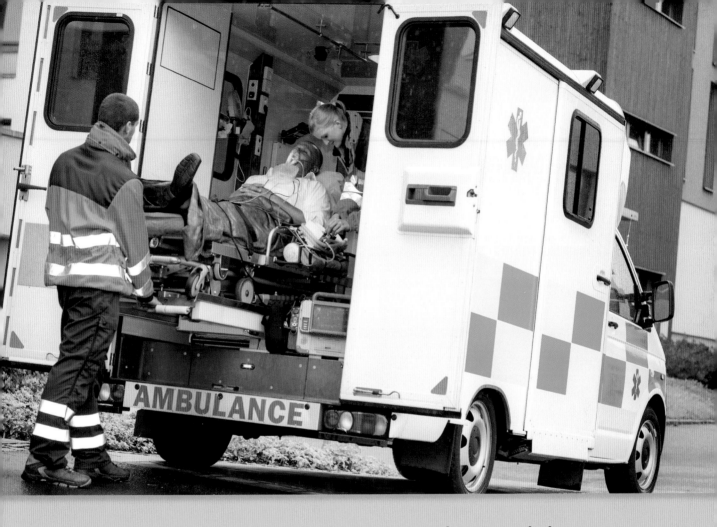

Today, some sick people get to
a hospital in an ambulance.

Medicine

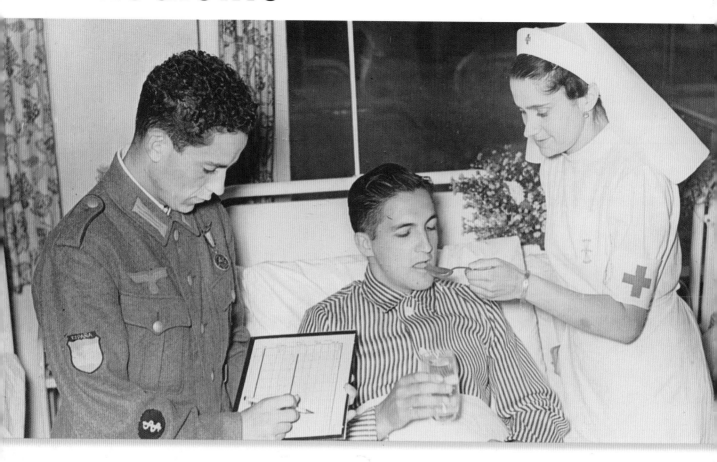

In the past doctors had few medicines to help sick people.

Today, there are many medicines
to help people get better.

15

Hospitals

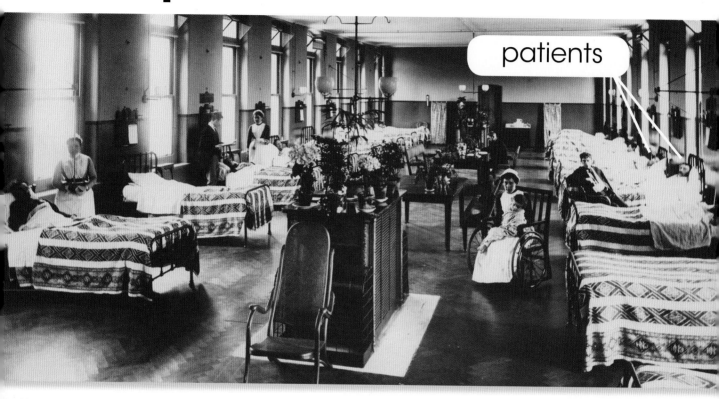

patients

In the past hospitals were made up of large rooms. Many patients stayed in the same room.

Today, hospitals are made up of many small rooms. Fewer patients stay in the same room.

Doctors and nurses

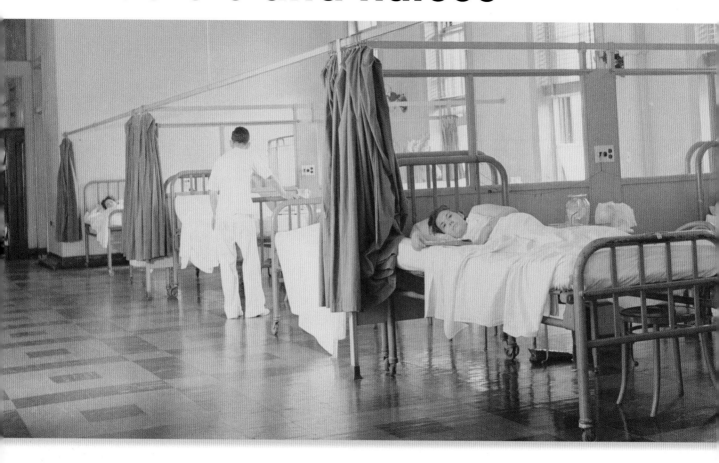

In the past hospitals had fewer

doctors.

Today, hospitals have many doctors.

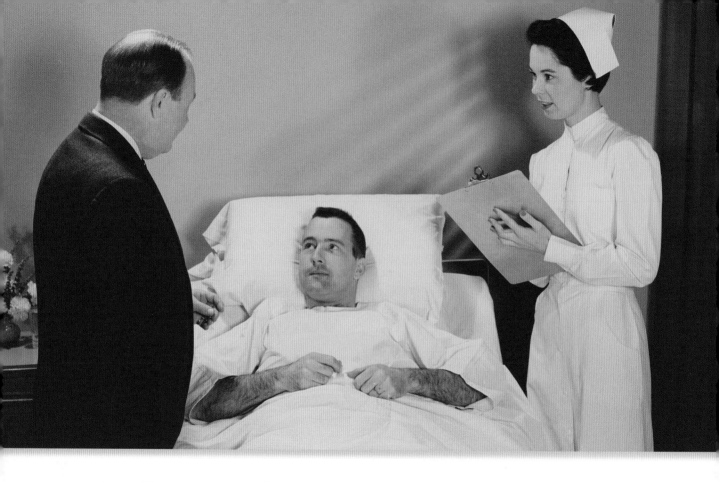

In the past nurses and doctors helped patients at the hospital.

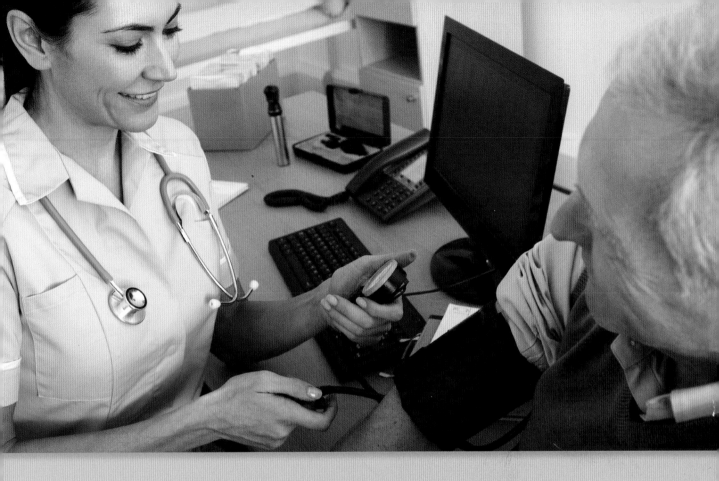

Today, nurses and doctors also
help patients at the hospital.

Then and now

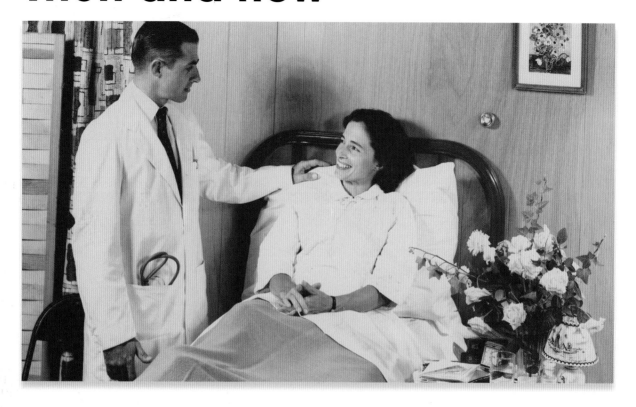

In the past doctors did their best to help sick patients. Today, doctors still

do their best to help sick patients.

Picture glossary

 **hospital** place where doctors and nurses work to care for patients

 **nurse** person who works in a hospital helping to care for patients

 **patient** person visiting a doctor for medicine or medical care

 **surgery** place where doctors see their patients

Index

ambulances 13

hospital 9, 11, 16, 17, 18, 19, 20, 23

medicines 14, 15

nurses 20, 21, 23

patients 16, 17, 20, 21, 22, 23

surgery 9, 11, 23

Notes for parents and teachers

Before reading

Teach children about the difference between the past and present. Explain to children that things that have already happened are in the past. To help them understand this concept, ask children to tell you about what they ate for breakfast. Then, explain to them that their breakfast happened in the past. Tell children that your conversation is happening in the present.

After reading

- Explain to children that the way people visit the doctor has changed over time. Ask children to describe their last visit to a doctor. Encourage them to think about driving to the doctor's surgery, whether they saw a nurse, and what the surgery looked like.

- Ask children to look at the images on pages 12–13. Can they think of any ways the images are different? Can they think of why it might be helpful to get to the hospital quickly?

- Show children the image on page 15. Explain that today, many medicines exist to help people heal from different sicknesses. Ask children how life in the past might have been more difficult with fewer medicines.